ANGEL'S ALPHABET

MARIE ANGEL

PELHAM BOOKS

First published in Great Britain by
Pelham Books Ltd
27 Wrights Lane
Kensington
London W8 5TZ
1986

British Library Cataloguing in Publication Data

Angel, Marie
  Angel's alphabet.
  1. English language — Alphabet — Juvenile
  literature
  1. Title
  421'.1 PE1155

  ISBN 0-7207-1715-9

Printed in Portugal by Printer Portuguesa, Sintra.

aAa

antbird

anteater ant

B b

butterfly
bushbaby

D d

duck
dog donkey

Ee

emu–wren
elephant-shrew

F f

frog fly
fennec fox

G g

gecko

genet

H h

hare

hoopoe

I i

ibis

ibex

J j

jay

jackal   jerboa

K k

kangaroo
koala kagu

L l

lovebirds
lemur lemming

Mm

monkey

Nn

nuthatch
numbat

owl
olingo

P p

parrot
penguin pig

Q q

quail

R r

rabbit
robin

S s

snail

stoat

Tt

toucan
tiger
tortoise

Uu
umbrella-bird

Vv

vicuna
vole

X x

x-ray fish

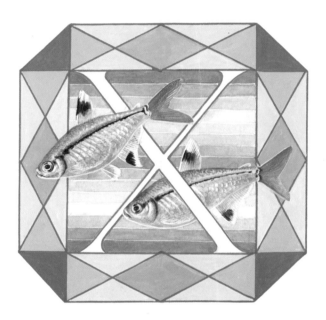

Yy

yellowhammer
yapok

Z z

zorilla

GLOSSARY

ANTBIRD (Spotted): South America: follows columns of army ants in the rain forests to feed on the insects.

ANTEATER (Giant): Central and South America: has a long sticky tongue to pick up ants and termites; it holds its large, bushy tail over its body for protection from sun or rain.

ANGELFISH: South America (River Amazon): flat, disc-shaped fish with black stripes and large, wing-like fins.

ELEPHANT-SHREW: South Africa: active day and night, it has a long trunk-like nose to push into cracks or crevices in search of food.

EMU-WREN: Australia: a curious little bird, its tail, which it holds upright, consists of six delicate feathers, longer in length than its body.

FENNEC FOX: North Africa: the smallest fox, but with huge ears; it digs a burrow in the desert sand and captures small reptiles, rodents and insects to eat.

GECKO: Corsica and Sardinia: unlike most reptiles, it can emit audible sounds which vary from chirps to barks. Its toe pads have minute hooks, which allow it to cling to most surfaces; geckos can run upside down across ceilings.

GENET: South-west Europe and Middle East: small member of the cat tribe; it lives in caves or rock crevices and hunts at night.

HOOPOE: Europe: named from the sound of its call. In mediaeval times hoopoes were linked with magic. Their long, curved bills probe for insects and grubs.

IBEX: Alps (above the treeline): has fine, long horns and a small beard. In the summer it grazes alpine meadows.

IBIS: Africa and Madagascar: a wandering bird of shore-line and marshes. Venerated in ancient Egypt.

JERBOA: Central Asia: a small nocturnal creature, it can make enormous leaps with its long hind legs. It digs burrows deep into the desert sand and eats seeds.

KAGU: New Caledonia: gives fantastic displays when excited, pulling its wings and tail feathers through its beak.

LEMUR (ring-tailed): Madagascar: has thick, soft fur and long ringed tail; although happy in trees, it spends much of its time on the ground, feeding on bark, grass and fruits.

NUMBAT: Australia: a small marsupial, it has a sticky tongue like an anteater, and feeds principally on ants. It has been known to eat as many as ten or twenty thousand a day.

OLINGO: Central and South America: mainly nocturnal, it spends most of its life in trees, rarely descending to the ground. Its long tail helps it to balance, as it runs and leaps along the branches.

UMBRELLA BIRD (ornate): Central and South America: crow-like bird with a crest which can be spread like a parasol. The bird also has an inflatable lappet of feathers hanging from its throat. It eats fruit.

VICUNA: South America: lives high up in the mountain peaks; its thick, woolly coat keeps out the cold.

YAPOK (Water Opossum): South America: a semi-aquatic animal, it has short, dense, seal-like fur. Its webbed feet enable it to move easily through the water and catch fish and crustaceans for food.

ZORILLA (Striped Polecat): Africa: normally nocturnal, it feeds on reptiles, rodents, birds' eggs and insects. During the day, it retreats to its burrow or a crevice in the rocks.

W w

wolf

widgeon